POEMS

FOR

MY

WIFE

A collection of poems celebrating love,
marriage and our first year of married life

by

Michael Cronogue

Poems For My Wife

Original copyright remains with the Author

Publisher: Lulu Publishing

Year of Publication: 2018

Email: michaelcronogue@gmail.com

ISBN: 978-0-244-96948-6

For Dawn

A collection of poems dedicated to the woman who is my everything in life and without whom I would not be the man I am today.

CONTENTS

Poems For My Wife

Dawn Elizabeth

Through all the years we have been as one
Life's many changes have made us both strong,
Your bright smile from the first time we met
Shone like a beacon, above all the rest.
Although there have been stumbles, our love never falters
Despite separations and imperfect solutions,
We care not for what others may humour
Challenges are faced, and overcome sooner.
As we head toward a decade of love
Sharing our hopes our dreams and our wishes
Onward we venture, never submission
Secure in our desires, our common ambitions.
Families grow up, so often to part
And new friendships replace those that have withered;
Despite all of this, our love it gets richer
Never taken for granted, always considered.
So on this day when all hearts should speak true
Here are my thoughts I give unto you:
So strong is our love, in times of plenty and strife
My Dawn Elizabeth, my love and my life

February 14th 2012

Love's Celebration

My love for you cannot be measured
In worldly things shorn of true meaning,
What I feel for you is mine to be treasured,
Amid the flow that is life's great teeming:
For the dozen years we have been as one
Through laughter, joy, tears and some sadness;
We can reminisce fondly about what we have done,
And reflect on a life that has brought us much gladness:
Like roses, a symbol of love's greater beauty
Your loveliness glows in its own special way,
You are my rock, my inspiration my own special Pucci,
My love for you grows stronger each day: so
On this the day which has such special meaning in life,
Would you please do me the honour, of becoming my wife?

For Dawn Elizabeth
June 15th 2014

Our Wedding Day

This is the day which for two years we have dreamt
As two become one, it is a sign of our commitment.
This celebration of love, so precious to you and me
Today my love in the sight of God, we enter into Holy Matrimony.

The sacred vows we make will signify our desire
Hearts forever entwined, flames of love burning even higher.
To those who could join us to commemorate our special day
Family and friends create the magic, which will never fade away.

As we exchange rings of marriage, symbols so simple and pure
We will honour and cherish each other, for our love it will endure.
But in the midst of this great joy let us take pause to remember, those
Now residing in heaven, who could not be here on this glorious September.

So as we set forth together joined in union as man and wife
We proceed on another great adventure, a further chapter in our life.
But for now my precious darling, these words I can finally say
All my love now and forever, on this, our Wedding Day.

To my darling Dawn on the day she makes me the happiest man alive
From your loving husband,
Michael
Saturday 10th September 2016

Six Week Anniversary

October brings many changes with leaf falls all around,
Outside the autumn breezes make for a beguiling sound.
It's six weeks to the day my love since you and I were wed;
Six weeks to the day my love, when our sacred vows we said.

With our friends and family already gathered near,
We spoke out clearly so that they might all hear.
To always love, honour and cherish, to unite in a single heart;
To always love, honour and cherish, so only death can us do part.

For our honeymoon we did travel to Kernow's northern shore,
Back to that tranquillity we have oft enjoyed before.
But this time it's with new purpose, this time it's with new life;
This time my precious darling, we travelled as man and wife.

Some said it might not feel different given the time we've been together,
But this feeling we have is so special we know it will last forever.
We know it will last forever, because my love we're strong;
We're strong my love for we're together, and proved the doubters wrong.

So on this October day as we return to our Cornish retreat,
The shadows of evening draw near the dog lying at our feet.
We count our blessings my darling more than words can ever impart;
We count our blessings my darling, as on married life we start.

Juliots Well
Camelford
23rd October 2016

November 14th – Our **Now Unofficial** Anniversary

Fourteen years have come around since on that first date we went, two career-obsessed individuals, still looking for that someone which makes life heaven-sent. A journey starting in Leeds from where text messages we had swapped, a quick call to a garage to clean the car and buy flowers, the only time I had stopped. Phoning ahead for directions for you to guide me through, that labyrinth called Clayhanger, to find the loveliness that was you. At a place called Sophia's, an Italian of some reputation, we wined, dined, laughed and talked, remaining oblivious to any other patron.

We both knew then we had something special, something we couldn't miss, though even after fourteen years we still disagree, on who actually leaned in for the initial kiss. So there it was my darling from that first date we set, but we agreed to keep it secret, for fear of our then-colleagues finding out just yet. But the memory I will always carry, the one I remember the most, was after I left you declared, that a certain someone was Toast!!

So every third Thursday in November, our hearts turn toward this special day, we've come a long way you and I so it only remains for me to say. If the Queen gets to celebrate two birthdays – and none more deserving than she – then you too my darling should also, have an official and unofficial, anniversary.

Our First **Unofficial** Anniversary
14th November 2016

The Gift of Love

What gift in life is more precious than this?
When two hearts are enjoined as one forever,
Through good times and bad we're always together
Since from that moment we shared love's first kiss.
A special feeling of contentment as on this day we start,
Our first married Christmas has finally come about;
And for you my darling let there be not any doubt
On this December morn, there's an extra zip in my heart.

As presents are exchanged and skype calls to family made,
We can pause and reflect on a truly memorable year
Our wedding, your new job and a future that seems clear;
Precious memories like these wrapped up never to fade
Do make this first married yuletide one to remember,
So this gift of love I give unto you, on this special day in December.

Our First Married Christmas
December 25th 2016

No January Blues For Me & You

New Year resolutions oft means new starts being made
Yet for some these are pledges already destined to fade.
For as we stand here still flushed with marital bliss,
My love and I won't be rushing into participating with this.
For we still live in the moment of that glorious glow,
That feeling of oneness such as only we can know.
Our New Year's resolution isn't this sense of new giving,
More the continuation of life, we have for a decade been living.

But there are some milestones in the year that's ahead
Some special firsts of which much will have to be said.
Valentine's, Easter, wedding anniversary to name but a few
Each takes on extra significance, in this year that's so new.
But with last September's memories still fresh in our views
Together we'll go forward, free from those January blues.

Our New, New Year
January 2017

Where it all Began

Five years ago on this very day
A poem to you I did compose,
Each heartfelt word in its own special way,
Carried an expression of love that everyone knows.
My first serious poem since my final school year,
But for you my darling, the memory's still clear.

Not in any sonnet form did I indeed write
Those words that my heart had conjured up to the fore,
Twenty lines of love half-rhyming yet tight,
My homage to the one that I truly adore.
In commemorating the martyrdom of a third century saint,
And capturing your loveliness like a masterpiece in paint.

February 14th has come around once more
And the feeling of love once again fills the sky,
But this year is different to the ones gone before,
For this day is extra special for my true love and I.
So I'll sign off this poem in my own unique way,
And wish my darling a happy, first married, St Valentine's Day.

To my own special Valentine
February 14th 2017

New Era is Dawn's

This day that has finally arrived

This day you have waited three months for,

Of ambitions you still hold deep inside,

For your talents to showcase once more.

While those left behind may regret

That you're moving on to pastures new,

Yet you always remember, never forget

Those who forever remained loyal to you.

You'd grown tired of foreign travel

Of internal squabbles and underhand tricks,

When the corporate plans begin to unravel,

Life became a daily game of politics.

Last December you had confirmation

That a new challenge would soon begin,

Once again it was further affirmation

Of your abilities and much more therein.

So come my love let us celebrate

Our continued year of glorious good morns,

For on this day let us not hesitate

To declare this new era is Dawn's.

First Day of a New Era
March 19th 2017

Easter Reflections

As this year of firsts continues onward
We arrive at that time that celebrates new growth,
An Easter season to reflect and to ponder
Those changes in life surrounding us both.
As we return once again to our Cornish retreat
To this place where much spiritual solace is sought,
The sun going down as the evening we greet
Precious times like these, just cannot be bought.

Good Friday coffee at St Julitta
Time to catch up with spiritual kin,
This medieval church each time I see her
Faith much reflected, in Celtic Christian origin.
We spend the weekend in our own company
Two people now joined together as one,
We play *Easter Parade* on an old DVD
Watching Fred dance with Judy, as we always have done.

Bank Holiday Monday a trip to Bodmin we take
To wander and explore its historic old streets,
Then off to Parkway for the train we must make
For the arrival of Katie, and her smile that's so sweet.
With her studies going well she's here for a rest
Casting the books to one side for some fresh Cornish air,
Veterinary nursing is her calling to be the very best
With her drive and dedication, she will surely get there.

When Tuesday comes round it's our last full day
And to Crackington Haven for lunch we make tracks,
A stroll along the cliff path looking out to the bay
The pebble beach below us, the fresh winds at our backs.
We return home via Bristol to Katie's student hall
Such a blessing to know that she's doing so well,
On our first married Easter we continue to walk tall
And from this new beginning, more tales of love we shall tell.

Cornwall
April 12th – 18th 2017

Whitsun Musings

Forty or so days since last Easter did dawn
To Camelford again we do wander,
To our Cornish retreat once more we are drawn
For the beauties of Whitsun to ponder.

Late spring brings forth its shimmering glory
With splashes of colour amid the bright greenery
Mother Nature's great bounty; that ultimate story,
Brings her characters to life in majestic scenery.

Our stay this time it is to be much shorter
Just three nights to read, relax and unwind,
The solace, the peace, like ripples on water
Creates an ambience so sweet, leaving worries behind.

We ventured to Launceston a long-held wish
And wandered aimlessly among its historic streets,
We sat and ate chips with freshly battered fish,
Taking great delight in these simple, yet magical treats.

As evenings drew near we watched sunsets sublime
Sink over the hills and the valleys below,
Glass of wine, a book, a magazine, down time
Our love for this place continues to grow.

The time to return home is upon us once more
As we pack the car up and prepare to depart,
We say our goodbyes as we shut and lock the door,
But in six short weeks my love, another adventure we start!

Camelford
Whitsun Bank Holiday 2017

Once in a Lifetime

The words on your card stood out so clear

They described so vividly my feelings for you,

No ordinary birthday in this memorable year

We celebrate together, for a love that is true.

Once in a lifetime the message declared

That something special that'll change things forever,

Meeting you my love could I have then dared

That our love would grow deeper, each day we're together.

You're the one that I will love forever

The one who I eulogise in rhyme,

For when we went out that special November

I knew I'd found my once-in-a-lifetime.

So to the one with whom I share this great life,

A very Happy Birthday, to my wonderful Wife.

On your first married birthday
June 15th 2017

Summer's Simplicities

The simple things in life are usually what's best
With the many ups and downs that put us to the test,
As we settle once again into our Cornish retreat,
It remains the perfect antidote that is always hard to beat.
A British summer holiday cannot in truth contest
With continental climates of sunshine and of zest,
Yet once again my love this place so warm and sweet
Provides the peaceful solitude, with which no other can compete.

Several times a year to the great South-West we head
But this time my love the more special are the steps we tread,
Marvelling at the sights and sounds of Kernow's northern reaches
As we stroll hand in hand, along those golden Cornish beaches.
In the evening twilight we mostly sat and talked or read
But sometimes there was no need for anything else to be said,
As we watched the sun sink behind the tall green beeches
We drank in the splendour, which Mother Nature graciously beseeches.

On Sunday afternoon we turned our attention toward sport
Watching the drama that unfolded live on Centre Court,
A plate of cream teas to the TV we both did bring
As Federer once again, showed why at Wimbledon he is King.
Such simple pleasures as these cannot ever be bought,
For it is these lessons in life which are always freely taught;
While others to materialism may desperately try to cling
Our strength is our bond, and is the key to everything.

Cornwall
July 09th – 19th 2017

Second (And Final) Time Around

Think back my love to that day last September
A day for many reasons, we will always certainly remember.
It was for me also a day that was most profound,
As I entered Holy Matrimony for the second time around.
Now some may become perplexed and afflicted by confusion
Wondering if happy married life can be more than just an illusion.
The reason I pose this question in case I forgot to mention,
Is that our current state of happiness, has made us
Objects of some close attention.

We'd been together a dozen years quite happily living over the brush
We knew we'd tie the knot one day so we weren't in any rush.
But when the time had come for us to formalise our union,
We didn't anticipate the obstacles,
Trying to enter into a loving communion.
Because there were a few things to contemplate
Which did indeed infuriate with those with whom perhaps,
We are now ready to commiserate.

Firstly changing of one's status, a most frustrating business
All the hoops you had to jump through, just to become a Mrs!
Passport, Driving Licence, Bank and Credit cards to mention a few
Then remembering just for convenience,
Your Facebook, Whatsapp & Twitter too.
Whatever family name you're changing,
Be it wife to husband's or sometimes husbands to wife,
Just going through the motions is the cause of so much strife.

As February 14th proved, being married can sometimes be hard
When seeking to buy my beloved that all-important St Valentine's card.
There's plenty for girlfriend, boyfriend, one I love & the love of my life,
Yet could I find a decent one, dedicated to my darling wife?
Yet despite all these recent obstacles, that could have blighted our way,
Based on recent experience I believe I'm in a position to say;

As we approach our first anniversary
I *can* make this statement profound;
Married life is certainly better,
When undertaken the second time round.

Bloxwich
August 2017

Our First Anniversary

Twelve months ago at the alter we stood
Our vows to each other we solemnly did say,
Twas twelve months ago on this very day
When we both said "I Do" as only we could.
Since on that day our married life we did start
Life has brought some interesting changes,
A reflection I feel on the things God arranges
To keep us together as one single heart.

This year of new starts in so many ways
Yet at times it feels like it's always been so,
But my Love and I in our hearts we both know
Our future together is more than years, months and days.
As we celebrate together our first year of married life
Happy Anniversary, to my most beautiful Wife.

Our First Anniversary
September 10th 2017

And Finally

This has been a true labour of love for all the right reasons.

For my Wife, Dawn; to be as blissfully happy together as we are after sixteen years through good times and sad times has been the source of inspiration for writing this book. You are my rock, my everything, for without you there would be no inspiration.

To our dog Bella, a true and loyal "Staffy" we cannot now remember what our life was like before you came into it. When we saw your picture on Birmingham Dogs Home website, Kennel no. 20 at Sunnyside with that tinsel around your neck, we knew you were the one for us.

Printed in Great Britain
by Amazon

34051406R10020